Introduction

The world of video game development is a landscape filled with creativity, innovation, and constant evolution. Yet, behind every beloved game lies a plethora of unseen versions and abandoned projects that never made it to the final release. These beta builds and unreleased games hold a treasure trove of insights into the development processes, the challenges faced by developers, and the creative decisions that shape the games we ultimately play. "Beta Builds and Lost Games: The Untold Stories of Video Game Development" aims to uncover these hidden gems, exploring their significance and the stories behind their creation and demise.

The Purpose of the Book

This book seeks to delve into the fascinating world of beta builds and unreleased video games, highlighting the crucial role they play in the broader narrative of game development. By examining these early versions, we gain a deeper understanding of the iterative nature of game design, where ideas are tested, refined, and sometimes discarded entirely. These beta versions often contain unique elements, gameplay mechanics, and storylines that provide a glimpse into the creative minds of developers and the direction a game might have taken.

Importance of Preserving Beta Builds

Preserving beta builds is not just about maintaining a record of what might have been; it's about preserving the history of an art form. Video games are a significant part of modern culture, and understanding their development is essential to appreciating their impact. Organizations like Hidden Palace and projects like Project Deluge have made significant strides in preserving these early versions, ensuring that future generations can study and appreciate the evolution of video games.

The process of developing a game is often complex and fraught with challenges. Developers must balance creative vision with technical feasibility, market demands, and the realities of production schedules. Beta builds represent a snapshot of this process, capturing moments of experimentation and innovation. They show us the pathways that were considered and the decisions that ultimately shaped the final product.

Notable Examples

Throughout this book, we will explore several notable beta builds and unreleased games, each with its own unique story. For instance, "12 Tales: Conker 64," an early version of what eventually became "Conker's Bad Fur Day," offers a fascinating case study of how a game can drastically change direction. Initially conceived as a family-friendly platformer, it was reimagined as a mature-themed game in response to market feedback and the creative vision of its developers.

Similarly, "Resident Evil 1.5," an early version of "Resident Evil 2," provides a compelling look at how a nearly completed game can be scrapped and reworked into something entirely different. The decision to restart the project led to significant improvements and ultimately resulted in one of the most beloved entries in the Resident Evil series.

The Role of Preservationists and Communities

The preservation of beta builds and unreleased games owes much to the dedicated efforts of preservationists and gaming communities. Platforms like Unseen64, PCGamingWiki, and community-driven projects have been instrumental in documenting, archiving, and sharing these early versions with the public. Their work ensures that these pieces of gaming history are not lost to time and provides invaluable resources for researchers, historians, and enthusiasts.

Preservation efforts are often a labor of love, driven by a passion for gaming and a commitment to historical accuracy. These communities work tirelessly to locate, restore, and share beta builds, often facing significant challenges such as deteriorating physical media, legal issues, and the sheer difficulty of finding these rare artifacts. Their contributions are vital to our understanding of game development and the preservation of digital heritage.

The Impact of Beta Builds on Modern Game Development

Studying beta builds offers valuable lessons for modern game development. They highlight the importance of iteration, the willingness to take risks, and the necessity of balancing creative vision with practical constraints. By examining these early versions, developers can gain insights into what works, what doesn't, and why certain decisions were made.

Moreover, beta builds and unreleased games serve as a source of inspiration. They remind us that innovation often comes from experimentation and that the path to success is rarely straightforward. Understanding the development process, with all its trials and errors, can inspire new generations of developers to push boundaries and explore new possibilities.

As we embark on this journey, we invite you to join us in uncovering the fascinating tales of beta builds and unreleased games. Together, we will explore the paths not taken, the innovations that emerged, and the legacy of these hidden gems in the world of video gaming.

Chapter 1: The World of Beta Builds

The journey of creating a video game is often shrouded in mystery and complexity, involving numerous iterations, creative decisions, and technical challenges. At the heart of this process are beta builds—early versions of games that offer a unique window into the developmental stages of video game design. These beta builds are not mere prototypes; they represent the evolving ideas, experimental gameplay mechanics, and artistic visions that developers explore before finalizing a game. This chapter delves into the world of beta builds, explaining what they are, their significance, and highlighting notable examples that illustrate their impact on the gaming industry.

Definition and Significance of Beta Builds

Beta builds, often referred to simply as "betas," are pre-release versions of software that are provided to a select group of users or testers to identify bugs, gather feedback, and test new features before the final release. In the context of video games, beta builds serve multiple purposes:

1. Testing and Feedback: Beta versions are crucial for identifying technical issues, gameplay imbalances, and user experience flaws. Testers, often including both internal teams and external volunteers, play these versions extensively to provide feedback that helps developers refine and polish the game.

2. Marketing and Hype: In many cases, beta builds are also used as marketing tools to generate excitement and anticipation for the game. By allowing fans to experience a taste of the game early, developers can build a community and create buzz that can significantly boost the game's profile ahead of its official launch.

3. Creative Exploration: Perhaps most intriguingly, beta builds reflect the iterative nature of game development. They showcase features, levels, characters, and storylines that may be significantly altered or entirely removed in the final product. This makes beta builds invaluable for understanding the creative process and the decisions that shape a game.

Historical Context of Beta Builds

The practice of releasing beta versions dates back to the early days of software development. However, in the realm of video games, it became more pronounced with the rise of home consoles and personal computers in the 1980s and 1990s. During this period, the complexity of games increased, and so did the need for extensive testing and feedback.

Early beta builds were often distributed on physical media such as floppy disks or CDs, shared among a small group of testers or gaming journalists. With the advent of the internet, the distribution of beta versions became more widespread and accessible, allowing developers to reach a larger audience and gather more diverse feedback.

Notable Beta Builds

Exploring notable beta builds offers insights into the development processes and the changes that games undergo before their final release. Here are a few examples that highlight the significance of beta builds in the gaming industry:

12 Tales: Conker 64

"12 Tales: Conker 64," initially known as "Conker's Quest," was announced at E3 1997 as a family-friendly platformer. Developed by Rare, the game was intended to follow the success of titles like "Banjo-Kazooie" by appealing to a younger audience. The gameplay featured Conker the Squirrel and his girlfriend Berri, who had different playstyles—Conker focused on action-oriented gameplay, while Berri used strategic elements such as commanding monsters.

However, criticism that the game was too similar to other platformers led Rare to drastically change its direction. The game was retooled and released as "Conker's Bad Fur Day" in 2001, with a mature theme that included adult humor, violence, and satirical content. The transformation from "12 Tales: Conker 64" to "Conker's Bad Fur Day" exemplifies how beta builds can reflect significant shifts in creative vision based on feedback and market considerations.

Resident Evil 1.5

Another fascinating example is "Resident Evil 1.5," an early version of "Resident Evil 2." Developed by Capcom, this version was nearly complete before being scrapped. The original concept featured Leon Kennedy, as in the final game, but paired him with Elza Walker, a motorcycle racer, instead of Claire Redfield. The environments included a more realistic Raccoon City Police Department and various industrial areas.

The decision to restart the project was driven by the desire to create a more dynamic and engaging game. The final version of "Resident Evil 2," released in 1998, featured significant improvements in graphics, gameplay, and storytelling. "Resident Evil 1.5" remains a highly sought-after artifact among fans, with partial builds leaking online and providing a glimpse into the development process.

Half-Life: Alpha Build

The alpha build of "Half-Life," leaked years after its development, provides an early look at what would become one of the most influential first-person shooters. This early version, known as Alpha 0.52, dated September 4, 1997, features different levels and mechanics that were significantly refined in the final release. The alpha build showcases the game's iterative development process and the enhancements made to deliver the groundbreaking experience that "Half-Life" is known for today.

S.T.A.L.K.E.R.: Shadow of Chernobyl

"Stalker: Shadow of Chernobyl" underwent numerous changes during its development, and its beta builds offer a fascinating glimpse into its evolution. The Pre-Alpha Build 1096 from 2002, for example, includes levels and gameplay elements that were either significantly altered or removed in the final game. The beta builds highlight the developers' experimentation with different gameplay mechanics and environmental designs, ultimately shaping the atmospheric and immersive experience of the final release.

GoldenEye 007

The beta build of "GoldenEye 007" for the Nintendo 64, known for its innovative multiplayer mode, included features and levels that were not present in the final version. Early prototypes showcased different mission structures and character models, providing insights into the development decisions that contributed to the game's success. The beta build highlights how iterative testing and feedback helped refine and perfect the gameplay mechanics that made "GoldenEye 007" a classic.

The Role of Preservationists and Communities

The preservation of beta builds and unreleased games owes much to the dedicated efforts of preservationists and gaming communities. Platforms like Unseen64 and PCGamingWiki have been instrumental in documenting, archiving, and sharing these early versions with the public. Their work ensures that these pieces of gaming history are not lost to time and provides invaluable resources for researchers, historians, and enthusiasts.

Preservation efforts are often a labor of love, driven by a passion for gaming and a commitment to historical accuracy. These communities work tirelessly to locate, restore, and share beta builds, often facing significant challenges such as deteriorating physical media, legal issues, and the sheer difficulty of finding these rare artifacts. Their contributions are vital to our understanding of game development and the preservation of digital heritage.

The Impact of Beta Builds on Modern Game Development

Studying beta builds offers valuable lessons for modern game development. They highlight the importance of iteration, the willingness to take risks, and the necessity of balancing creative vision with practical constraints. By examining these early versions, developers can gain insights into what works, what doesn't, and why certain decisions were made.

Moreover, beta builds and unreleased games serve as a source of inspiration. They remind us that innovation often comes from experimentation and that the path to success is rarely straightforward. Understanding the development process, with all its trials and errors, can inspire new generations of developers to push boundaries and explore new possibilities.

Beta builds are more than just early versions of games; they are a testament to the creative and technical journey that developers undertake. They offer a unique glimpse into the evolution of video games, showcasing the decisions, experiments, and changes that shape the final product. By preserving and studying these beta builds, we gain a deeper appreciation for the art and science of game development, and we ensure that the rich history of this medium is not lost to time. As we explore the stories behind these beta builds, we uncover the hidden gems of the gaming world and celebrate the innovation and creativity that drive this ever-evolving industry.

Chapter 2: The Evolution and Legacy of 12 Tales: Conker 64

The story of "12 Tales: Conker 64" is one of the most intriguing and well-documented examples of a game that underwent significant transformation during its development. Initially conceived as a family-friendly platformer, it ultimately became "Conker's Bad Fur Day," a game known for its mature themes and satirical content. This chapter explores the developmental history, the creative decisions, and the legacy of this unique game.

Early Development and Concept

"12 Tales: Conker 64" was announced at E3 1997, developed by Rare, a company renowned for its successful titles like "Donkey Kong Country" and "Banjo-Kazooie." The game was initially titled "Conker's Quest" and was designed to be a cheerful, colorful platformer aimed at a younger audience. It followed the adventures of Conker the Squirrel and his girlfriend Berri, with gameplay focused on exploration, puzzle-solving, and combat.

The game's initial design featured two distinct playstyles: Conker's action-oriented gameplay with a slingshot as his primary weapon and Berri's more strategic approach, where she could command monsters to assist her. The world of "12 Tales: Conker 64" was vibrant and whimsical, filled with various enemies, environmental puzzles, and numerous collectibles. This design aimed to capture the charm and success of other platformers of the era.

The Shift in Direction

Despite its promising start, "12 Tales: Conker 64" faced criticism for being too similar to other Rare titles, particularly "Banjo-Kazooie." This feedback, combined with an industry trend toward more mature gaming experiences, prompted Rare to reconsider the direction of the game. The development team, led by Chris Seavor, decided to overhaul the game's concept entirely.

By 1999, the game had been reimagined as "Conker's Bad Fur Day." This new direction was a bold departure from its original family-friendly design, embracing adult humor, satire, and mature themes. The decision was partly influenced by the desire to stand out in a crowded market and to address the perception of the Nintendo 64 as a console primarily for children
Development Challenges and Changes

Transforming "12 Tales: Conker 64" into "Conker's Bad Fur Day" was no small feat. The development team had to overhaul nearly every aspect of the game, from its storyline and characters to its gameplay mechanics and visual style. The cheerful, colorful environments were replaced with darker, more detailed settings that complemented the game's mature tone.

One of the most significant changes was the narrative. The story of "Conker's Bad Fur Day" centered on Conker's misadventures after a night of heavy drinking, filled with parodies of popular movies, crude humor, and satirical takes on various aspects of culture and gaming. This new narrative required extensive rewrites and new voice acting, much of which was provided by Chris Seavor himself.

Gameplay mechanics also saw significant revisions. While the core platforming elements remained, new mechanics were introduced to support the game's more complex and varied levels. These included context-sensitive actions, where Conker could interact with different objects and environments in specific ways depending on the situation, adding depth and variety to the gameplay.

Reception and Legacy

"Conker's Bad Fur Day" was released on March 5, 2001, toward the end of the Nintendo 64's life cycle. Despite its critical acclaim, particularly for its humor, voice acting, and bold design choices, the game struggled commercially. Several factors contributed to this, including limited marketing, its mature rating, and the declining popularity of the Nintendo 64 as the industry transitioned to newer consoles.

However, over the years, "Conker's Bad Fur Day" has achieved cult status. Its unique blend of humor, satire, and solid gameplay has earned it a dedicated fanbase and a significant place in gaming history. The game was re-released on the Xbox in 2005 as "Conker: Live & Reloaded," featuring updated graphics and an online multiplayer mode, though it received mixed reviews due to some censorship and changes from the original.

The Legacy of 12 Tales: Conker 64

The story of "12 Tales: Conker 64" and its transformation into "Conker's Bad Fur Day" highlights several important aspects of game development:

1. Creative Flexibility: The willingness of the development team to completely overhaul the game in response to feedback and market trends showcases the importance of adaptability and creative flexibility in game development.

2. Market Trends: The shift from a family-friendly platformer to a mature-themed game reflects broader industry trends and the evolving demographics of gamers. This change also underscores the challenges developers face in balancing creative vision with commercial viability.

3. Cultural Impact: "Conker's Bad Fur Day" remains a notable example of how video games can push boundaries and explore themes that were considered taboo at the time. Its success in this regard paved the way for future games to tackle more mature and diverse subjects.

4. Preservation of Game History: The journey of "12 Tales: Conker 64" to "Conker's Bad Fur Day" also highlights the importance of preserving different stages of game development. Early builds, concept art, and developer notes provide valuable insights into the creative process and the evolution of the game.

Rediscovery and Documentation

Interest in "12 Tales: Conker 64" has persisted over the years, fueled by glimpses of early builds and concept art shared by former Rare employees and game preservationists. In 2012, a 30-minute gameplay video of "12 Tales: Conker 64" surfaced on YouTube, showing Conker navigating through levels that never made it into the final game. This footage provided a fascinating look at the game's original design and the extensive changes it underwent.

Moreover, in March 2023, Tim Stamper, co-founder of Rare, shared footage of a working development cartridge via social media. This footage included scenes from the game's title sequence and gameplay, confirming that "12 Tales: Conker 64" remains intact within the Rare archives. These discoveries have reignited interest in the game's development history and the creative decisions behind its transformation.

The evolution of "12 Tales: Conker 64" into "Conker's Bad Fur Day" is a compelling story of creative risk-taking, adaptability, and the impact of market forces on game development. It illustrates the challenges and rewards of pushing boundaries and reimagining a project to create something truly unique. The legacy of this transformation continues to inspire developers and gamers alike, reminding us of the innovative spirit that drives the video game industry. As we delve deeper into the world of beta builds and unreleased games, the story of "12 Tales: Conker 64" serves as a testament to the rich, often unpredictable journey from concept to final product.

Chapter 2: The Evolution and Legacy of 12 Tales: Conker 64

The story of "12 Tales: Conker 64" is one of the most intriguing and well-documented examples of a game that underwent significant transformation during its development. Initially conceived as a family-friendly platformer, it ultimately became "Conker's Bad Fur Day," a game known for its mature themes and satirical content. This chapter explores the developmental history, the creative decisions, and the legacy of this unique game.

Early Development and Concept

"12 Tales: Conker 64" was announced at E3 1997, developed by Rare, a company renowned for its successful titles like "Donkey Kong Country" and "Banjo-Kazooie." The game was initially titled "Conker's Quest" and was designed to be a cheerful, colorful platformer aimed at a younger audience. It followed the adventures of Conker the Squirrel and his girlfriend Berri, with gameplay focused on exploration, puzzle-solving, and combat.

The game's initial design featured two distinct playstyles: Conker's action-oriented gameplay with a slingshot as his primary weapon and Berri's more strategic approach, where she could command monsters to assist her. The world of "12 Tales: Conker 64" was vibrant and whimsical, filled with various enemies, environmental puzzles, and numerous collectibles. This design aimed to capture the charm and success of other platformers of the era.

The Shift in Direction

Despite its promising start, "12 Tales: Conker 64" faced criticism for being too similar to other Rare titles, particularly "Banjo-Kazooie." This feedback, combined with an industry trend toward more mature gaming experiences, prompted Rare to reconsider the direction of the game. The development team, led by Chris Seavor, decided to overhaul the game's concept entirely.

By 1999, the game had been reimagined as "Conker's Bad Fur Day." This new direction was a bold departure from its original family-friendly design, embracing adult humor, satire, and mature themes. The decision was partly influenced by the desire to stand out in a crowded market and to address the perception of the Nintendo 64 as a console primarily for children.

Development Challenges and Changes

Transforming "12 Tales: Conker 64" into "Conker's Bad Fur Day" was no small feat. The development team had to overhaul nearly every aspect of the game, from its storyline and characters to its gameplay mechanics and visual style. The cheerful, colorful environments were replaced with darker, more detailed settings that complemented the game's mature tone.

One of the most significant changes was the narrative. The story of "Conker's Bad Fur Day" centered on Conker's misadventures after a night of heavy drinking, filled with parodies of popular movies, crude humor, and satirical takes on various aspects of culture and gaming. This new narrative required extensive rewrites and new voice acting, much of which was provided by Chris Seavor himself.

Gameplay mechanics also saw significant revisions. While the core platforming elements remained, new mechanics were introduced to support the game's more complex and varied levels. These included context-sensitive actions, where Conker could interact with different objects and environments in specific ways depending on the situation, adding depth and variety to the gameplay.

Reception and Legacy

"Conker's Bad Fur Day" was released on March 5, 2001, toward the end of the Nintendo 64's life cycle. Despite its critical acclaim, particularly for its humor, voice acting, and bold design choices, the game struggled commercially. Several factors contributed to this, including limited marketing, its mature rating, and the declining popularity of the Nintendo 64 as the industry transitioned to newer consoles.

However, over the years, "Conker's Bad Fur Day" has achieved cult status. Its unique blend of humor, satire, and solid gameplay has earned it a dedicated fanbase and a significant place in gaming history. The game was re-released on the Xbox in 2005 as "Conker: Live & Reloaded," featuring updated graphics and an online multiplayer mode, though it received mixed reviews due to some censorship and changes from the original.

The Legacy of 12 Tales: Conker 64

The story of "12 Tales: Conker 64" and its transformation into "Conker's Bad Fur Day" highlights several important aspects of game development:

1. Creative Flexibility: The willingness of the development team to completely overhaul the game in response to feedback and market trends showcases the importance of adaptability and creative flexibility in game development.

2. Market Trends: The shift from a family-friendly platformer to a mature-themed game reflects broader industry trends and the evolving demographics of gamers. This change also underscores the challenges developers face in balancing creative vision with commercial viability.

3. Cultural Impact: "Conker's Bad Fur Day" remains a notable example of how video games can push boundaries and explore themes that were considered taboo at the time. Its success in this regard paved the way for future games to tackle more mature and diverse subjects.

4. Preservation of Game History: The journey of "12 Tales: Conker 64" to "Conker's Bad Fur Day" also highlights the importance of preserving different stages of game development. Early builds, concept art, and developer notes provide valuable insights into the creative process and the evolution of the game.

Rediscovery and Documentation

Interest in "12 Tales: Conker 64" has persisted over the years, fueled by glimpses of early builds and concept art shared by former Rare employees and game preservationists. In 2012, a 30-minute gameplay video of "12 Tales: Conker 64" surfaced on YouTube, showing Conker navigating through levels that never made it into the final game. This footage provided a fascinating look at the game's original design and the extensive changes it underwent.

Moreover, in March 2023, Tim Stamper, co-founder of Rare, shared footage of a working development cartridge via social media. This footage included scenes from the game's title sequence and gameplay, confirming that "12 Tales: Conker 64" remains intact within the Rare archives. These discoveries have reignited interest in the game's development history and the creative decisions behind its transformation.

The evolution of "12 Tales: Conker 64" into "Conker's Bad Fur Day" is a compelling story of creative risk-taking, adaptability, and the impact of market forces on game development. It illustrates the challenges and rewards of pushing boundaries and reimagining a project to create something truly unique. The legacy of this transformation continues to inspire developers and gamers alike, reminding us of the innovative spirit that drives the video game industry. As we delve deeper into the world of beta builds and unreleased games, the story of "12 Tales: Conker 64" serves as a testament to the rich, often unpredictable journey from concept to final product.

Chapter 4: Other Notable Beta Builds and Unreleased Games

The world of video game development is filled with stories of projects that never saw the light of day or were drastically altered from their original vision. While some games, like "12 Tales: Conker 64" and "Resident Evil 1.5," have garnered significant attention, there are many other beta builds and unreleased games that offer fascinating insights into the creative process and the challenges faced by developers. This chapter explores several other notable examples, highlighting their development histories, the reasons behind their cancellations or changes, and their legacies.

Fireteam Rogue

"Fireteam Rogue" was a promising action-adventure game developed by Accolade for the Super Nintendo Entertainment System (SNES). Announced in the early 1990s, the game aimed to blend elements of platforming, shooting, and role-playing, set in a sci-fi universe where players would control a team of elite soldiers fighting against alien threats.

Despite an ambitious start and a strong narrative, "Fireteam Rogue" faced numerous development challenges. The project was marred by poor management, technical difficulties, and constant delays. The development team struggled to implement the game's innovative ideas, such as its branching storylines and cooperative gameplay mechanics. Eventually, these issues led to the game's cancellation, leaving behind a tantalizing glimpse of what could have been through preview articles and promotional materials.

"Fireteam Rogue" serves as a cautionary tale about the importance of effective project management and the risks of overambition in game development. The lessons learned from its development have informed subsequent projects, emphasizing the need for clear vision, robust planning, and adaptability in the face of technical challenges.

S.T.A.L.K.E.R.: Shadow of Chernobyl

"S.T.A.L.K.E.R.: Shadow of Chernobyl" is a renowned first-person shooter developed by GSC Game World. The game's development history is marked by numerous changes and delays, with beta builds revealing a significantly different vision from the final product. The early versions of "S.T.A.L.K.E.R." featured more extensive RPG elements, different environments, and various gameplay mechanics that were altered or removed during development.

One of the most notable beta builds is the Pre-Alpha Build 1096 from 2002. This version included levels and features that showcased the game's early direction, such as more detailed environmental interactions and a greater focus on survival elements. However, due to technical limitations and the need to streamline the gameplay, many of these features were scaled back or reworked in the final release.

The beta builds of "S.T.A.L.K.E.R." highlight the iterative nature of game development and the need to balance ambitious ideas with practical constraints. The game's final version was ultimately well-received, praised for its atmosphere and immersive world, but the beta builds offer a fascinating glimpse into the project's evolution.

GoldenEye 007

"GoldenEye 007" for the Nintendo 64 is a landmark title in the history of first-person shooters, but its development was not without its challenges. The beta builds of the game reveal several features and levels that were altered or cut from the final version. Early prototypes included different mission structures, character models, and gameplay mechanics that were refined through extensive testing and feedback.

One of the most significant changes was the game's multiplayer mode. Initially, the multiplayer component was not part of the original plan and was added late in development. The beta builds show various iterations of this mode, including different maps and weapon configurations. The final version's multiplayer became one of its most celebrated features, showcasing how iterative testing can lead to significant improvements.

The story of "GoldenEye 007" underscores the importance of flexibility and responsiveness in game development. The ability to adapt and refine gameplay elements based on testing and feedback played a crucial role in the game's success, making it a classic that continues to influence the genre.

Hannibal: The Game

"Hannibal: The Game" was an ambitious project by Arxel Tribe, intended to be an adaptation of the film "Hannibal" directed by Ridley Scott. The game was designed to put players in the role of FBI agent Clarice Starling as she tracks down the infamous Hannibal Lecter. The developers aimed to create a deeply immersive experience, combining elements of psychological horror, investigation, and action.

Despite its promising concept, "Hannibal: The Game" faced numerous development hurdles. The project struggled with funding issues, technical challenges, and creative disagreements. These problems led to significant delays and ultimately the game's cancellation. Only a few screenshots and concept art remain, providing a glimpse into what could have been a unique addition to the horror genre.

The cancellation of "Hannibal: The Game" highlights the difficulties in adapting complex narratives into interactive experiences. The project's ambitious scope and the challenges it faced underscore the importance of clear vision, strong leadership, and adequate resources in game development.

Duke Nukem Forever

"Duke Nukem Forever" is infamous for its protracted development cycle, which spanned over 15 years. Initially announced in 1997, the game faced numerous delays, engine changes, and development team overhauls. The beta builds of "Duke Nukem Forever" showcase various iterations of the game, each reflecting different stages of development and design philosophies.

The early versions of "Duke Nukem Forever" featured different levels, weapons, and gameplay mechanics compared to the final release. These beta builds reveal the ambitious scope of the project and the many challenges the development team faced in bringing their vision to life. Despite finally being released in 2011, the game received mixed reviews, with many critics noting its dated design and inconsistent quality.

The tumultuous development of "Duke Nukem Forever" serves as a cautionary tale about the risks of extended development cycles and the impact of changing technologies and market expectations on a game's final outcome. It underscores the importance of setting realistic goals and maintaining a clear direction throughout the development process.

Legacy of Beta Builds and Unreleased Games

The stories of these beta builds and unreleased games offer valuable lessons and insights into the complexities of game development. They highlight the importance of iteration, flexibility, and effective project management, as well as the challenges of balancing creative vision with practical constraints. Moreover, they underscore the significance of preserving these early versions to understand the evolution of video games and the creative processes behind them.

The efforts of preservationists and gaming communities in documenting and restoring these beta builds ensure that these important pieces of gaming history are not lost. By studying these early versions, developers and enthusiasts can gain a deeper appreciation for the art and science of game development, learning from the successes and failures of past projects.

As we continue to explore the world of beta builds and unreleased games, we uncover the hidden gems of the gaming industry, celebrating the innovation, creativity, and perseverance that drive the creation of video games. These stories remind us that the path to success is rarely straightforward and that every game, whether released or not, contributes to the rich tapestry of the medium's history.

Chapter 5: The Role of Preservationists and Communities

The preservation of beta builds and unreleased games is a crucial aspect of understanding and appreciating the history and evolution of video games. This chapter explores the efforts of dedicated preservationists and communities in documenting, archiving, and sharing these early versions. It also highlights the challenges they face, the importance of their work, and the impact of their contributions on the gaming industry and beyond.

The Importance of Preservation

Preserving beta builds and unreleased games is not just about maintaining a record of what might have been; it's about preserving the history of an art form. Video games are a significant part of modern culture, and understanding their development is essential to appreciating their impact. Preservation efforts ensure that future generations can study and appreciate the evolution of video games, learn from past successes and failures, and draw inspiration for future innovations.

Key Players In Preservation

Several key players and organizations have made significant contributions to the preservation of beta builds and unreleased games. These include dedicated individuals, fan communities, and specialized organizations that work tirelessly to locate, restore, and share these valuable pieces of gaming history.

1. Hidden Palace and Project Deluge

Hidden Palace is a community-driven organization dedicated to the preservation of video game prototypes, beta builds, and unreleased titles. One of their most notable initiatives, Project Deluge, has uncovered and shared nearly 500 prototypes and unreleased games, including significant finds such as a playable version of Rare's unreleased N64 game "Dinosaur Planet" and a fully playable "GoldenEye Xbox Live Arcade" build. These discoveries provide a unique glimpse into the development processes and creative decisions behind some of the industry's most iconic titles.

2. Unseen64

Unseen64 is an extensive archive of beta builds, canceled games, and unreleased projects. The site is maintained by a team of volunteers who document and share information, screenshots, and videos of these early versions. Unseen64 covers a wide array of titles from different eras and platforms, preserving valuable insights into the history of game development. Examples include "Fireteam Rogue," "Hannibal: The Game," and many others, showcasing the diverse range of projects that have been abandoned or significantly altered over the years.

3. PCGamingWiki

PCGamingWiki is a collaborative website that focuses on documenting and fixing PC games, but it also plays a crucial role in preserving beta builds and unreleased games. The site provides detailed information on various leaked versions, such as "Half-Life Alpha 0.52," "Doom 3 E3 Demo Alpha," and "S.T.A.L.K.E.R.: Shadow of Chernobyl Pre-Alpha Build 1096." By archiving these early versions, PCGamingWiki ensures that they are accessible to researchers, historians, and enthusiasts who want to explore the development history of these titles.

4. The Lost Media Wiki

The Lost Media Wiki is another important resource for preserving beta builds and unreleased games. It focuses on documenting and archiving lost, obscure, or unreleased media, including video games. The site provides detailed articles on various projects, such as "12 Tales: Conker 64," offering valuable insights into their development and eventual fate.

Challenges in Preservation

Preserving beta builds and unreleased games is a challenging endeavor that requires significant effort, resources, and dedication. Some of the key challenges faced by preservationists include:

1. Deteriorating Physical Media: Many early beta builds and prototypes were stored on physical media such as floppy disks, CDs, and cartridges. Over time, these media can degrade, making it difficult to access and preserve the data they contain. Preservationists must often employ specialized techniques and equipment to recover and digitize these materials before they are lost forever.

2. Legal Issues: The preservation and sharing of beta builds and unreleased games can raise legal concerns, particularly with regard to intellectual property rights. Developers and publishers may have proprietary interests in these early versions, leading to potential conflicts over their distribution and use. Preservationists must navigate these legal complexities to ensure that their efforts are both ethical and compliant with relevant laws and regulations.

3. Funding and Resources: Preservation efforts require significant financial and logistical support. From acquiring rare materials to maintaining servers and storage facilities, the costs associated with preserving beta builds and unreleased games can be substantial. Many preservationists rely on donations, crowdfunding, and volunteer work to sustain their activities.

4. Technical Challenges: Recovering and restoring beta builds often involves overcoming technical challenges, such as corrupted data, incomplete files, and outdated formats. Preservationists must possess a high level of technical expertise and access to specialized tools to address these issues and ensure that the preserved materials are usable and accessible.

Impact of Preservation Efforts

The work of preservationists and communities has had a profound impact on the gaming industry and beyond. Their contributions have helped to:

1. Enrich Gaming History: By preserving beta builds and unreleased games, preservationists provide valuable insights into the development processes, creative decisions, and technological advancements that have shaped the gaming industry. These preserved materials enrich our

understanding of gaming history and offer a deeper appreciation for the art and science of game development.

2. Inspire Future Innovations: Studying beta builds and unreleased games can inspire future innovations by showcasing the iterative nature of game design and highlighting both successful and unsuccessful experiments. Developers can learn from the past, drawing inspiration from the ideas and techniques explored in these early versions.

3. Foster Community Engagement: Preservation efforts foster a sense of community among gaming enthusiasts, historians, and researchers. By sharing their findings and collaborating on restoration projects, preservationists create opportunities for meaningful engagement and collective learning.

4. Promote Ethical Practices: The work of preservationists highlights the importance of ethical practices in game development and archiving. By documenting and sharing their methods, they promote transparency, accountability, and respect for intellectual property rights.

The preservation of beta builds and unreleased games is a vital endeavor that ensures the rich history of video game development is not lost to time. The dedicated efforts of preservationists and communities provide invaluable insights into the creative processes, challenges, and innovations that have shaped the gaming industry. By overcoming technical, legal, and financial challenges, these passionate individuals and organizations safeguard the legacy of video games and inspire future generations of developers and enthusiasts.

As we continue to explore the world of beta builds and unreleased games, we celebrate the tireless work of preservationists and the enduring impact of their contributions. Their efforts remind us of the importance of preserving our cultural heritage and the transformative power of video games as an art form and a medium of expression.

Chapter 6: The Impact of Beta Builds on Modern Game Development

Beta builds and unreleased games offer a unique window into the creative process and technical challenges of video game development. Studying these early versions provides valuable lessons for modern developers, highlighting the importance of iteration, risk-taking, and balancing creative vision with practical constraints. This chapter explores the various ways in which beta builds have influenced contemporary game development and the broader gaming industry.

Lessons in Iteration and Refinement

One of the most critical lessons beta builds teach is the importance of iteration and refinement in game development. The iterative process involves creating, testing, and refining various aspects of a game to enhance its quality and appeal. Beta builds often serve as a tangible record of this process, showcasing the evolution of gameplay mechanics, storylines, and visual designs.

For example, the transformation of "Resident Evil 1.5" into "Resident Evil 2" demonstrates how significant changes can lead to a more polished and engaging final product. The decision to restart the project allowed Capcom to refine the game's narrative, improve its graphical fidelity, and enhance its gameplay mechanics, resulting in a title that became a cornerstone of the survival horror genre.

Similarly, the development of "S.T.A.L.K.E.R.: Shadow of Chernobyl" illustrates how iterative testing can lead to substantial improvements. Early beta builds revealed ambitious features and complex environments that were eventually streamlined to create a more cohesive and immersive experience. These iterations helped the developers strike a balance between their creative vision and the practical limitations of their technology.

Encouraging Risk-Taking and Innovation

Beta builds often contain experimental features and bold design choices that may not make it into the final release. These elements highlight the willingness of developers to take risks and explore new ideas during the development process. Studying these early versions can inspire modern developers to embrace experimentation and push the boundaries of game design.

For instance, "12 Tales: Conker 64" initially aimed to be a family-friendly platformer but was transformed into the mature-themed "Conker's Bad Fur Day." This radical shift in direction showcased Rare's willingness to take creative risks and redefine the game's identity to stand out in a crowded market. The result was a unique and memorable game that continues to be celebrated for its boldness and originality.

Similarly, the various iterations of "GoldenEye 007" demonstrate how incorporating feedback and making significant changes can lead to innovative gameplay experiences. The addition of the multiplayer mode, which was not part of the original plan, became one of the game's most iconic features. This willingness to adapt and innovate during the development process contributed to the game's lasting legacy.

Balancing Creative Vision and Practical Constraints

Beta builds also highlight the challenges developers face in balancing their creative vision with practical constraints such as technological limitations, budgetary concerns, and market demands. Understanding these constraints and how developers navigate them can provide valuable insights for modern game development.

The story of "Duke Nukem Forever" serves as a cautionary tale about the impact of extended development cycles and changing technologies. The game's numerous beta builds reflect various stages of development, each showcasing different design philosophies and technological approaches. Ultimately, the protracted development period led to a final product that struggled to meet contemporary expectations. This example underscores the importance of setting realistic goals and maintaining a clear direction throughout the development process.

On the other hand, the development of "Half-Life" and its alpha builds reveal how developers can effectively manage constraints to create a groundbreaking experience. Valve's iterative approach allowed them to refine the game's mechanics, narrative, and level design, resulting in a title that set new standards for the first-person shooter genre. By studying these early versions, modern developers can learn how to balance ambition with feasibility to achieve their creative goals.

Preserving and Learning from Game History

The preservation of beta builds and unreleased games plays a crucial role in understanding the history and evolution of video game development. These early versions provide valuable insights into the creative processes, technical challenges, and industry trends that have shaped the medium. By studying preserved beta builds, developers can gain a deeper appreciation for the art and science of game development.

Organizations like Hidden Palace, Unseen64, and PCGamingWiki have made significant contributions to the preservation of beta builds and unreleased games. Their efforts ensure that these important pieces of gaming history are accessible to researchers, historians, and enthusiasts. This preservation work also helps to highlight the iterative nature of game development and the importance of learning from past projects.

Moreover, the preservation of beta builds fosters a sense of community among gaming enthusiasts and developers. By sharing their findings and collaborating on restoration projects, preservationists create opportunities for collective learning and engagement. This sense of community helps to celebrate the rich history of video games and promotes a deeper understanding of the medium.

Inspiring Future Generations of Developers

Studying beta builds and unreleased games can inspire future generations of developers by showcasing the creative potential and challenges of game development. These early versions highlight the importance of perseverance, adaptability, and innovation in the face of obstacles. Aspiring developers can learn valuable lessons from the successes and failures of past projects, drawing inspiration for their own creative endeavors.

The story of "Resident Evil 1.5" and its impact on "Resident Evil 2" serves as a powerful example of how embracing change and iterating on ideas can lead to significant improvements. Similarly, the evolution of "12 Tales: Conker 64" into "Conker's Bad Fur Day" demonstrates the value of bold creative decisions and the willingness to redefine a project's direction.

By preserving and studying beta builds, modern developers can gain insights into the complexities of game development and the importance of balancing creativity with practicality.

These lessons can help to foster a culture of innovation and excellence within the industry, encouraging developers to push the boundaries of what is possible in video games.

The impact of beta builds on modern game development is profound and far-reaching. These early versions provide valuable insights into the iterative nature of game design, the importance of risk-taking and innovation, and the challenges of balancing creative vision with practical constraints. By studying and preserving beta builds, developers can learn from the past and draw inspiration for future innovations.

The efforts of preservationists and gaming communities play a crucial role in safeguarding the history and evolution of video games. Their work ensures that these important pieces of gaming history are not lost to time and that future generations can continue to learn from and be inspired by the rich legacy of video game development.

As we continue to explore the world of beta builds and unreleased games, we celebrate the creativity, perseverance, and innovation that drive the medium forward. These stories remind us that the path to success is rarely straightforward and that every game, whether released or not, contributes to the rich tapestry of the gaming industry's history. Through the preservation and study of beta builds, we can continue to honor the past while inspiring the future of video game development.

Appendices

List of Notable Beta Builds and Unreleased Games

1. 12 Tales: Conker 64

   - Developer: Rare

   - Platform: Nintendo 64

   - Initial Concept: A family-friendly platformer featuring Conker the Squirrel and his girlfriend Berri.

   - Significant Changes: Transformed into "Conker's Bad Fur Day" with mature themes and adult humor.

- Legacy: Demonstrates the impact of market feedback and the willingness to take creative risks.

2. Resident Evil 1.5

   - Developer: Capcom

   - Platform: PlayStation

   - Initial Concept: Early version of "Resident Evil 2" featuring Leon S. Kennedy and Elza Walker.

   - Significant Changes: Restarted and redesigned, leading to the final version of "Resident Evil 2" with Claire Redfield replacing Elza Walker.

   - Legacy: Highlights the importance of iteration and refinement in game development.

3. Fireteam Rogue

   - Developer: Accolade

   - Platform: Super Nintendo Entertainment System (SNES)

   - Initial Concept: A sci-fi action-adventure game combining platforming, shooting, and role-playing elements.

   - Significant Changes: Cancelled due to development challenges, including poor management and technical difficulties.

   - Legacy: Serves as a cautionary tale about the risks of overambition and the need for effective project management.

4. S.T.A.L.K.E.R.: Shadow of Chernobyl

   - Developer: GSC Game World

   - Platform: PC

   - Initial Concept: A first-person shooter with extensive RPG elements and detailed environments.

   - Significant Changes: Early beta builds featured different levels and mechanics that were streamlined in the final release.

- Legacy: Demonstrates the iterative nature of game development and the balance between ambition and feasibility.

5. GoldenEye 007

   - Developer: Rare

   - Platform: Nintendo 64

   - Initial Concept: A first-person shooter based on the James Bond film, with a focus on single-player missions.

   - Significant Changes: Addition of a multiplayer mode late in development, which became one of the game's most celebrated features.

   - Legacy: Highlights the importance of flexibility and responsiveness to feedback in game development.

6. Hannibal: The Game

   - Developer: Arxel Tribe

   - Platform: PC

   - Initial Concept: An adaptation of the film "Hannibal," featuring FBI agent Clarice Starling tracking Hannibal Lecter.

   - Significant Changes: Cancelled due to funding issues, technical challenges, and creative disagreements.

   - Legacy: Emphasizes the challenges of adapting complex narratives into interactive experiences.

7. Duke Nukem Forever

   - Developer: 3D Realms, Gearbox Software

   - Platform: PC, PlayStation 3, Xbox 360

   - Initial Concept: A follow-up to "Duke Nukem 3D" with enhanced graphics and gameplay.

   - Significant Changes: Underwent numerous delays, engine changes, and development team overhauls over 15 years.

- Legacy: Serves as a cautionary tale about the risks of extended development cycles and changing technologies.

Resources and Further Reading

1. Hidden Palace

   - A community-driven organization dedicated to the preservation of video game prototypes, beta builds, and unreleased titles.

   - Website: hiddenpalace.org

2. Unseen64

   - An extensive archive of beta builds, canceled games, and unreleased projects, maintained by a team of volunteers.

   - Website: unseen64.net

3. PCGamingWiki

   - A collaborative website that documents and fixes PC games, including information on various leaked versions.

   - Website: pcgamingwiki.com

4. The Lost Media Wiki

   - A resource for documenting and archiving lost, obscure, or unreleased media, including video games.

   - Website: lostmediawiki.com

Acknowledgments

This book would not have been possible without the contributions of numerous individuals and organizations dedicated to preserving the history of video game development. Special thanks go to the following:

1. Hidden Palace Community

   - For their tireless efforts in uncovering and sharing beta builds and unreleased games through initiatives like Project Deluge.

2. Unseen64 Team

   - For their comprehensive documentation and preservation of beta builds and canceled games, providing invaluable insights into the development processes of many iconic titles.

3. PCGamingWiki Contributors

   - For their detailed and collaborative work in archiving information about leaked versions and providing a platform for fixing and improving PC games.

4. Lost Media Wiki Contributors

   - For their dedication to preserving lost and obscure media, including video games, and making this information accessible to the public.

5. Gaming Communities and Fans

   - For their passion and support in preserving and celebrating the history of video games. Your enthusiasm and contributions help keep the legacy of these early versions alive.

6. Game Developers and Industry Professionals

   - For sharing their experiences, insights, and materials related to the development of beta builds and unreleased games. Your openness and willingness to contribute to the preservation of gaming history are deeply appreciated.

Through the collective efforts of these individuals and organizations, we can continue to explore, understand, and appreciate the rich history of video game development. Their work ensures that the stories behind beta builds and unreleased games are not lost to time and that future generations can learn from and be inspired by the creative processes that shape the medium.

www.ingramcontent.com/pod-product-compliance
Lightning Source LLC
Chambersburg PA
CBHW082242220526
45479CB00005B/1311